NATURAL DISASTERS

TSUNAMIS

ABDO
Publishing Company

Rochelle Baltzer

Big Buddy BOOKS
Natural Disasters

VISIT US AT
www.abdopublishing.com

Published by ABDO Publishing Company, 8000 West 78th Street, Edina, Minnesota 55439.

Printed in the United States of America, North Mankato, Minnesota.
052011
092011

PRINTED ON RECYCLED PAPER

Coordinating Series Editor: Sarah Tieck
Contributing Editors: Megan M. Gunderson, BreAnn Rumsch, Marcia Zappa
Graphic Design: Adam Craven
Cover Photograph: *AP Photo*: Choo Youn-kong, Pool.
Interior Photographs/Illustrations: *AP Photo*: Dita Alangkara (p. 27), U.S.Navy, Jordan R. Beesley/HO (p. 25), Family Photo (p. 27), Marco Garcia (p. 21), Katsumi Kasahara (p. 23), Rob Lawson/PRNewsFoto/SAIC (p. 21), Natacha Pisarenko (p. 13), Yomiuri Shimbun (p. 29); *Getty Images*: Paula Bronstein (p. 19), PORNCHAI KITTIWONGSAKUL/AFP (p. 27); *iStockphoto*: ©iStockphoto.com/Aero17 (p. 23), ©iStockphoto.com/drnadig (p. 7); *Photo Researchers, Inc.*: Sally Bensusen (p. 9), Chris Butler (p. 9), New York Public Library (p. 17); *Photolibrary*: The Medical File/Marcia Hartsock (p. 15), Peter Arnold Images (p. 7), Still Pictures (p. 5); *Shutterstock*: Norma Cornes (p. 11), robootb (p. 25), Kochnera Tetyana (p. 30).

Library of Congress Cataloging-in-Publication Data

Baltzer, Rochelle, 1982-
  Tsunamis / Rochelle Baltzer.
    p. cm. -- (Natural disasters)
  ISBN 978-1-61783-034-1
  1. Tsunamis--Juvenile literature. 2. Tsunami damage--Juvenile literature. I. Title.
  GC221.5.B35 2012
  363.34'94--dc22
                      2011012763

TSUNAMIS

CONTENTS

POWERFUL TSUNAMIS

Deep under the ocean, an **earthquake** shakes the seafloor. Waves begin to roll out. They get taller and taller as they push toward land. It's a tsunami!

A tsunami (soo-NAH-mee) is a natural disaster. Natural disasters happen because of weather or changes inside Earth. They may **damage** land and buildings. Sometimes, they take lives. Learning about them helps people stay safe.

BREAKING NEWS

The word *tsunami* comes from two Japanese words. *Tsu* means "harbor" and *nami* means "wave."

Tsunamis can flood coasts, wiping away beaches and homes.

WAVE TRAIN

A tsunami is a group of ocean waves known as a wave train. Tsunami waves are different from regular ocean waves. Regular waves are mostly caused by wind.

Most tsunamis are caused by underwater **earthquakes**. They can also happen after underwater **landslides** and volcanic eruptions. These events can **displace** a large amount of water. This causes waves to travel out in a circle.

Imagine tossing a stone into a pond. Ripples move out from where you tossed it. That is similar to how a tsunami spreads.

A volcanic eruption is when hot liquid rock or steam comes out of a deep opening, or vent, in Earth's surface. This can happen on land or underwater.

WALLS OF WATER

Tsunami waves can travel very fast. In deep water, they move up to 500 miles (800 km) per hour!

As the waves enter shallow water, they slow down and get taller. When they hit land, the waves may look like walls of water!

BREAKING NEWS

Far out at sea, tsunami waves are usually less than three feet (1 m) high. And, they can be more than one hour apart. So, ships don't often notice them.

A tsunami wave can be taller than some buildings!

WAVE TRAIN

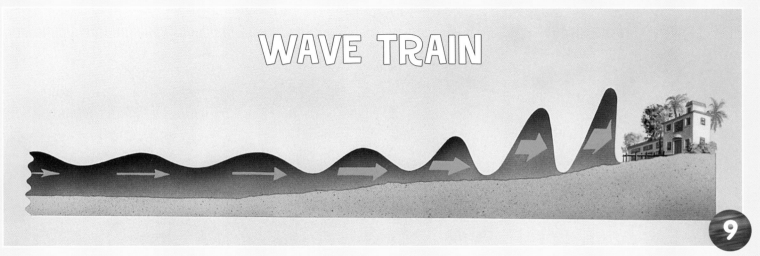

WAVE AFTER WAVE

Sometimes, the lowest part of a tsunami wave hits land first. When this happens, water draws far back from the shore. This is a warning. The highest part of the wave is on its way!

Tide affects how much water draws back from a beach (*below*). But before some tsunamis, much more of the seafloor shows.

BREAKING NEWS

Tsunamis used to be called tidal waves. But, they are not connected to ocean tides. So, they are no longer called that.

Once a tsunami wave hits land, it travels until its **energy** runs out. A wave may move across land for several hundred feet. As it travels, it picks up and moves things in its path. This includes boats, large rocks, and pieces of buildings.

The first wave is not always the largest in the wave train. That means danger can last for a while. The next wave might hit shore five minutes or an hour later. So, a tsunami can last for several hours.

Tsunamis are very powerful.
They can move large
objects, such as boats.

13

IN THE ZONE

Tsunamis can strike any low coastal area. Most happen in the Pacific Ocean. The Ring of Fire outlines most of the Pacific Ocean. Many volcanoes are in the Ring of Fire. Many **earthquakes** also occur there. So, tsunamis are likely.

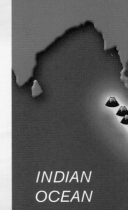

INDIAN OCEAN

BREAKING NEWS

Tsunami waves can cross the Pacific Ocean in less than a day!

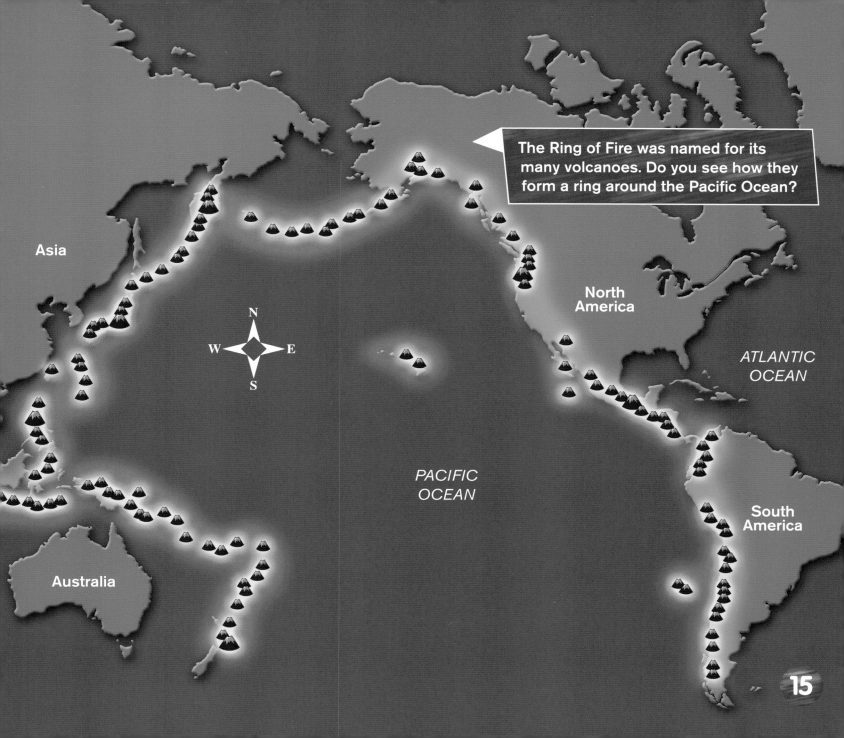

The Ring of Fire was named for its many volcanoes. Do you see how they form a ring around the Pacific Ocean?

15

DAMAGE AND DESTRUCTION

Tsunamis can cause a lot of **damage**. They destroy buildings and roads. They also flood land. This can ruin farmland and dirty a water supply.

Tsunamis also hurt natural areas. They can badly harm **coral reefs** and swamps. And, they often wash sea animals up on shore. Tsunamis can reshape entire coasts.

before

In 2004, a tsunami struck in the Indian Ocean. It flooded and reshaped nearby coasts.

after

RESCUE ME!

Tsunamis can be powerful enough to carry people out to sea. Many times, people drown in the waves. **Rescue** teams get to work after a tsunami hits. They bring people to safety.

Tsunamis often leave areas filled with **debris**. So, people work together to clean up and rebuild communities.

Underwater tsunami debris can be a danger to animals, plants, and boats. So, divers help clean it up.

19

PREDICTING TSUNAMIS

An underwater **earthquake** is a warning of a tsunami. Scientists use tools called seismographs (SIZE-muh-grafs) to measure earthquakes. They can **predict** the size, place, and time of possible tsunamis.

Another tool lies on the ocean floor. It measures changes in water **pressure** and sends the data to a buoy (BOO-ee). The buoy then sends the data to a warning center. The warning center notifies officials, newspeople, and the public.

The United States has two warning centers. The Pacific Tsunami Warning Center is in Hawaii (*right*). Another center is in Alaska.

Tsunami buoys float in oceans around the world. They are common in areas with a lot of tsunamis, such as the Ring of Fire.

21

SAFETY LESSON

In places where tsunamis are common, people work to keep the area safe. Coasts often have seawalls. These lessen the force of a tsunami when it hits shore.

Communities also have safety plans. If a warning is given, people go to higher ground away from rivers or streams.

Marked paths or roads are the safest, fastest ways to reach safety.

Seawalls are built strong. They are meant to keep towns and cities safe from tall waves.

CASE STUDY:
INDIAN OCEAN TSUNAMI

On December 26, 2004, a very strong **earthquake** shook the Indian Ocean. It was off the coast of the Indonesian island of Sumatra. It led to a powerful tsunami.

Before the tsunami struck, water drained from some beaches. Then, giant waves began to roll ashore. They crashed through beaches, farmland, villages, and cities.

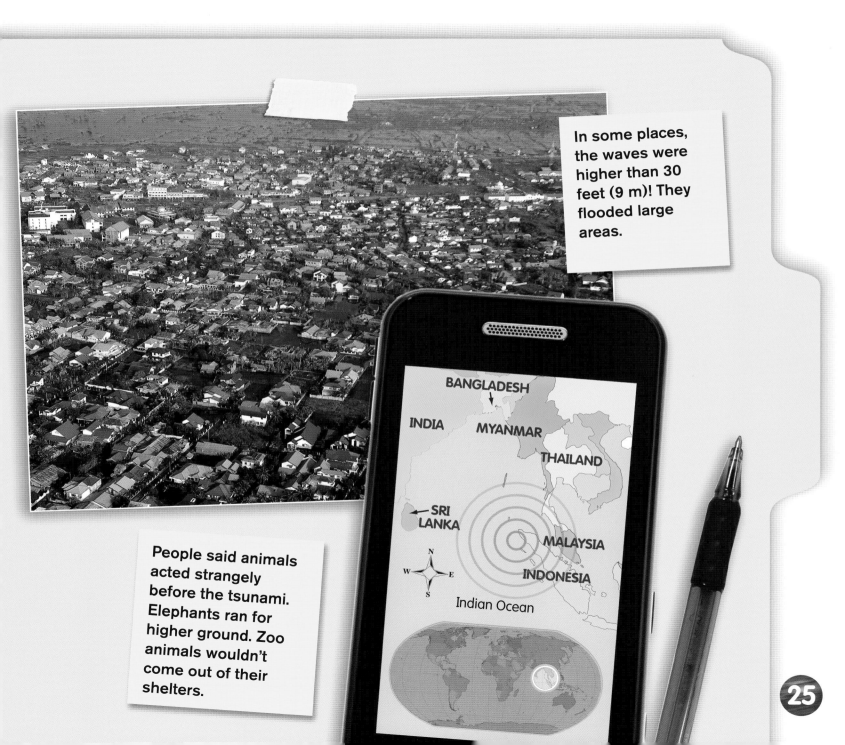

In some places, the waves were higher than 30 feet (9 m)! They flooded large areas.

People said animals acted strangely before the tsunami. Elephants ran for higher ground. Zoo animals wouldn't come out of their shelters.

BANGLADESH

INDIA

MYANMAR

THAILAND

SRI LANKA

MALAYSIA

INDONESIA

N
W E
S

Indian Ocean

The tsunami took just seven hours to spread through the Indian Ocean. It **damaged** more than ten countries in Southern Asia and Eastern Africa. Buildings, bridges, and roads were ruined.

The tsunami killed more than 200,000 people. It left others homeless. Many countries gave money, food, water, and clothing to help.

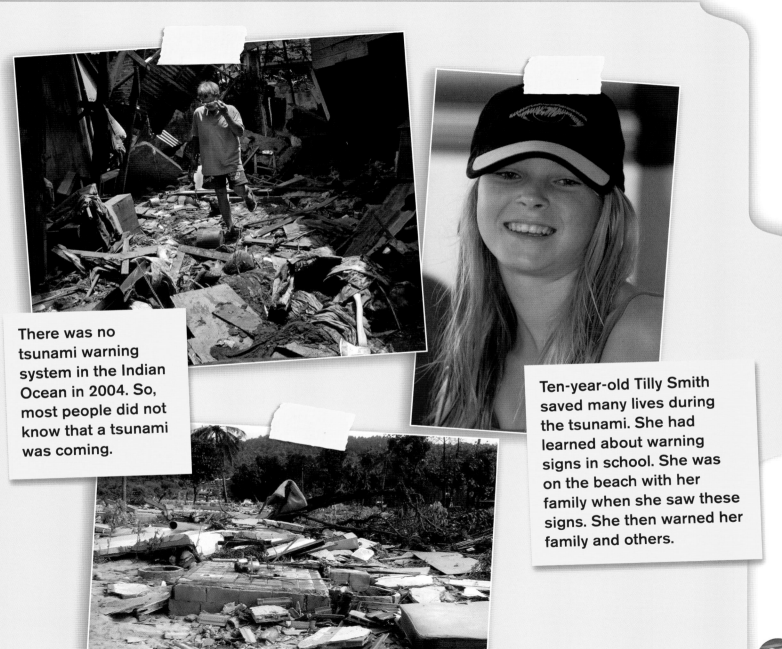

There was no tsunami warning system in the Indian Ocean in 2004. So, most people did not know that a tsunami was coming.

Ten-year-old Tilly Smith saved many lives during the tsunami. She had learned about warning signs in school. She was on the beach with her family when she saw these signs. She then warned her family and others.

FORCE OF NATURE

Tsunamis are one of Earth's powerful forces. Some are small and do not cause much harm. Others result in much **damage**. Scientists continue to study tsunamis. They find new ways to improve safety and prevent harm. This can save lives!

In March 2011, a tsunami hit Japan after a big earthquake. Water tore through land, moving boats, cars, trucks, and even houses.

は ま ゆ

BREAKING NEWS

Towns and cities were washed away after the Japan earthquake and tsunami of 2011. Tens of thousands of people were killed.

NEWS FLASH!

- In the United States, Hawaii, Alaska, California, Oregon, and Washington are most likely to be affected by a tsunami.

- Tsunamis can happen in the day or night, during any season, and in all weather.

- On average, two **damaging** tsunamis happen each year in the Pacific Ocean.

- Nature has its own way of guarding against tsunamis. **Coral reefs** weaken tsunamis. Bays, sand dunes, river entrances, and thick trees also do this.

IMPORTANT WORDS

coral reef a natural underwater structure made up of coral. Coral is a hard material formed from the remains of small sea creatures.

damage (DA-mihj) harm or injury. To damage is to cause harm or injury.

debris (duh-BREE) bits and pieces of something broken down or wrecked.

displace to move from the usual place or position.

earthquake (UHRTH-kwayk) a shaking of a part of the earth.

energy (EH-nuhr-jee) usable power. Heat is one form of energy.

landslide a mass of soil or rock that slides down a slope.

predict to say something is going to happen before it does.

pressure (PREH-shuhr) the pushing of a force against an opposing force.

rescue (REHS-kyoo) to save from danger or harm.

WEB SITES

To learn more about tsunamis, visit ABDO Publishing Company online. Web sites about tsunamis are featured on our Book Links page. These links are routinely monitored and updated to provide the most current information available.

www.abdopublishing.com

INDEX